Chinese Americans

by Joseph Gustaitis

Series Consultant: Judith A. Warner, Ph.D., Professor of Sociology and Criminal Justice, Texas A&M International University

Marshall Cavendish
Benchmark
New York

Marshall Cavendish Benchmark
99 White Plains Road
Tarrytown, NY 10591
www.marshallcavendish.us

Library of Congress Cataloging-in-Publication Data

Gustaitis, Joseph Alan, 1944-
    Chinese Americans / by Joseph Gustaitis.
       p. cm. — (New Americans)
    Includes bibliographical references and index.
    ISBN 978-0-7614-4303-2
    1. Chinese Americans—Juvenile literature. 2. Chinese
    Americans—History—Juvenile literature. I. Title.
    E184.C5G876 2010
    973'.04951—dc22   2009003170

Developed for Marshall Cavendish Benchmark by RJF Publishing LLC
Robert Famighetti, President
www.RJFpublishing.com
Design: Westgraphix LLC/Tammy West
Photo Research: Edward A. Thomas
Map Illustrator: Stefan Chabluk
Index: Nila Glikin

Cover: Street life in San Francisco's Chinatown, one of the oldest
Chinese-American communities.

Printed in Malaysia.

135642

CONTENTS

Words defined in the glossary are in **bold** type
the first time they appear in the text.

INTRODUCTION

The United States has embraced immigration for most of its history—and has been a destination of choice for people seeking a better life. Today hundreds of thousands of immigrants arrive each year to live and work and make their way in a new country. These "New Americans" come for many reasons, and they come from places all over the world. They bring with them new customs, languages, and traditions—and face many challenges in their adopted country. Over time, they and their children are changed by and become part of the American mainstream culture. At the same time, the mainstream is itself changed as it absorbs many elements of the immigrants' cultures, from ethnic foods to ideas from non-Western belief systems. An understanding of the New Americans, and how they will form part of the American future, is essential for everyone.

This series focuses on recent immigrants from eight major countries and regions: the Caribbean and Central America, China, India and other South Asian countries, Korea, Mexico, Russia and Eastern Europe, Southeast Asia, and West Africa.

Each of these geographic areas is a major source of the millions of immigrants who have come to the United States in the last decades of the twentieth century and the beginning of the twenty-first. For many of these people, the opportunity to move to the United States was opened up by the major

New Americans being sworn in as U.S. citizens.

changes in U.S. immigration law that occurred in the 1960s. For others, the opportunity or imperative to immigrate was triggered by events in their own countries, such as the collapse of Communism in Eastern Europe or civil wars in Central America.

Some of the New Americans found sizable communities of Americans from the same ethnic background and had the benefit of "ethnic neighborhoods" to move into where they could feel welcome and get help adjusting to American life. Many of these communities originated in a previous major wave of immigration, from the 1880s to 1920. Some of the New Americans found very few predecessors to ease the transition as they faced the challenges of adjustment.

These volumes tell the stories of the New Americans, including the personal accounts of a number of immigrants and their children who agreed to be interviewed by some of the authors. As you read, you will learn about the countries of origin and the cultures of these newcomers to American society. You will learn, as well, about how the New Americans are enriching, as they adapt to, American life.

Judith A. Warner, Ph.D.
Professor of Sociology and Criminal Justice
Texas A&M International University

Among the many ways Chinese culture has influenced
American life: Chinese food is one of the most
popular kinds of food among people
of all backgrounds.

CHAPTER ONE

THE CHINESE-AMERICAN COMMUNITY TODAY

Have you ever eaten wonton soup or chicken chow mein? Has someone you know taken **kung fu** lessons? Maybe you've seen the movie *Kung Fu Panda*. Maybe you've watched figure skating on TV and have seen Michelle Kwan. These are just a few examples of the many ways that Chinese culture and Chinese Americans are a part of American life today.

By the Numbers

Chinese Americans are one of the fastest-growing immigrant groups. In 2006, more than 3 million people of Chinese origin were living in the United States. Many Chinese immigrants come from the mainland of China. However, many others come from the offshore island of Taiwan (which has a different government from mainland China's)

China, Taiwan, and Hong Kong

In the late 1940s, China was in a civil war. On one side were the **Communists**, and on the other side were the Nationalists. (The United States supported the Nationalists.) The Communists won and took over China in October 1949. The Nationalists then set up their own government on the island of Taiwan, which is about 90 miles (140 kilometers) off the coast of China.

Today, China has a population of more than 1.3 billion people; it has more people than any other country. Taiwan has a population of about 23 million people. Taiwan has never declared itself an independent country. The Chinese government considers Taiwan a part of China.

Hong Kong is a region on the coast of southern China. It includes Hong Kong Island, other nearby islands, and a small area of land on the mainland. Its population is about 7 million. Until 1997, Hong Kong had been a British colony for about 150 years. In the second half of the twentieth century, the people of Hong Kong had greater personal, political, and economic freedom than the Communist Chinese government generally allowed on the mainland, and Hong Kong had a strong economy. When Great Britain agreed to return Hong Kong to China, some Hong Kong Chinese immigrated to the United States (as well as to Great Britain and elsewhere) because they were concerned about losing their freedoms and prosperity. To ease such concerns, when it took control of Hong Kong on July 1, 1997, the Chinese government made Hong Kong a "special administrative region." The government agreed to allow Hong Kong a great deal of autonomy (or self-rule), so that it could continue pre-1997 practices. This special status for Hong Kong is sometimes called "one country, two systems."

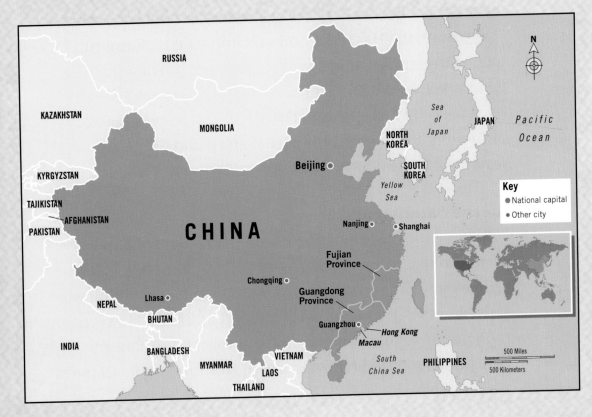

or from Hong Kong (which has a special status within China). About 70 percent of Chinese Americans were born outside the United States. More than half of the Chinese immigrants in the United States in 2006 arrived since 1990. In the 1990s, an average of 42,000 **documented immigrants** came to the United States from China each year.

More than half of all Chinese Americans live in just two states: California and New York. Texas, New Jersey, Massachusetts, and Illinois also had more than 100,000 Chinese-American residents in 2006, according to U.S. Census Bureau estimates. Chinese neighborhoods, called Chinatowns, are found in or near the centers of many large U.S. cities, including New York City, Los Angeles, San Francisco, Chicago, Houston, Philadelphia, San Diego, Dallas, San Antonio, and Detroit. In states with significant numbers of Chinese Americans, many suburban towns also have large Chinese communities. New immigrants often first head for such "ethnic neighborhoods," where people speak their language, stores carry familiar products, and it can be generally easier for the immigrants to settle in and begin life in a new country.

Success and Struggle

According to the Census Bureau, Chinese Americans, as a group, are economically successful in the United States. Many are well paid, working in such areas as business, technology, and medicine. More than half of all Chinese American workers have professional jobs of this kind, compared to about one-third of all American workers. Chinese

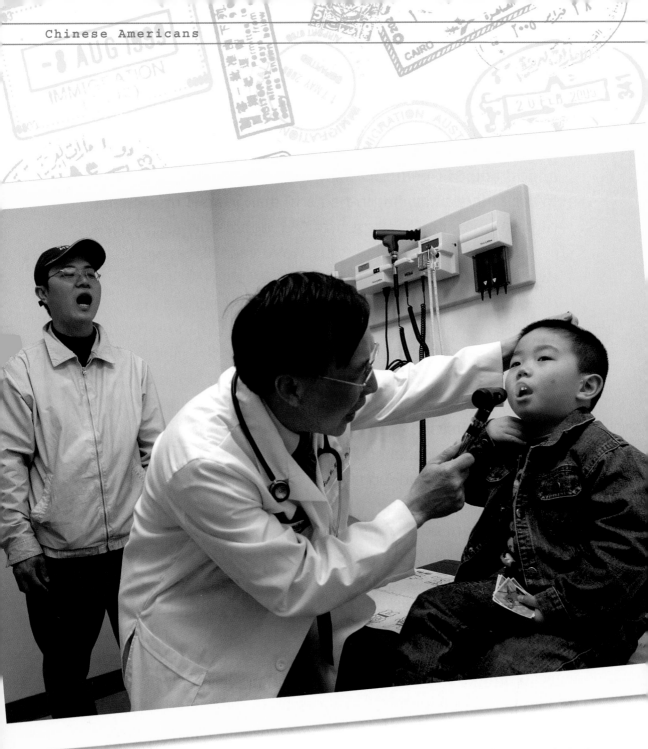

Many Chinese Americans are highly skilled professionals. Here, a doctor examines a young patient, while the father coaches the boy in how to say "ah."

Americans also tend to be well educated. More than half of Chinese Americans twenty-five years of age and older have a college or graduate school degree, compared to only about 27 percent of all American adults. So it is not surprising that the median income of Chinese-American families was more than $75,000 a year in 2006—almost $17,000 higher than the median income for all American families.

But these statistics don't tell the whole story. In 2006, 12 percent of Chinese Americans lived in poverty (as defined by the U.S. government). Chinese Americans work in such low-paying occupations as restaurant worker, store clerk or cashier, and garment worker (someone who makes clothing). In some places, Chinese Americans, most of them women, work in what are known as **sweatshops**. These are usually clothing factories where the hours are long, the working conditions are poor, and the pay is low. Often the owners of these factories break the laws that limit working hours, require a minimum hourly pay, and require a safe place to work. The sweatshop workers often include **undocumented immigrants,** who have entered the United States without obtaining the necessary U.S. government approvals and documents. Undocumented immigrants may be afraid to complain to government agencies about problems with their jobs. They don't want to call attention to themselves and risk being forced to leave the United States.

The Chinese Family

As with any immigrant group, there are differences—and sometimes tensions—between the Chinese-American

States with the Most Chinese Americans

California	1,165,605
New York	519,672
Texas	136,377
New Jersey	129,896
Massachusetts	114,638
Illinois	104,266
Washington	81,636
Pennsylvania	72,622
Maryland	67,351
Florida	65,743

Source: U.S. Bureau of the Census, 2006 estimates

immigrant parents who came to the United States as adults and their children who were either born in the United States or arrived at a very young age. Some of the tensions may relate to language. More than 80 percent of Chinese Americans do not regularly speak English at home, according to Census Bureau estimates. Some immigrant parents may find it hard to learn English, and those who live in Chinatowns may feel less of a need to learn a great deal of English. In fact, in one survey, almost half of all Chinese Americans said that they did not speak English very well. But the children of immigrants usually pick up English more quickly, especially when they go to school. This means that children often have to explain or translate things to their parents. This reversal of the typical parent-child role can be a source of tension.

Traditionally, the Chinese family is closer knit than other American families, and Chinese parents tend to be stricter with their children. For example, it is not considered appropriate for a child to leave home before getting married. Historically, some Americans have looked down on Chinese immigrants, and this has caused some immigrants to feel a need to stick together even more. But Chinese-American children watch American television, go to American movies, make friends who are not Chinese, and may be quicker to adopt and accept American culture, even while their parents may not think that American ways of doing things are the best. The process of trying to work out these family tensions is part of the process of Chinese-American **assimilation** into American life.

Chinese immigrants try to strike it rich in the California Gold Rush of the mid-1800s.

CHAPTER TWO

EARLIER GENERATIONS

It's hard to say when the first Chinese came to North America. Some historians think that in 1571 the Spanish brought Chinese shipbuilders to California, which was then ruled by Spain. But in the early 1900s, when a special committee of Congress called the Immigration Commission studied past immigration to the United States, it concluded that in 1820 the Chinese-American population of the United States was exactly one person.

The history of Chinese immigration to the United States can be divided into three parts:

- **1820–1882:** This was a period of unrestricted immigration. Any Chinese who wanted to could come to the United States. At times, Chinese men were even encouraged to immigrate because there was a shortage of workers in the American West.

- **1882–1943:** This was a period of restriction. Laws were passed in the United States prohibiting almost all immigration from China. Chinese Americans sometimes refer to this time as the "Silent Decades."
- **1943 and After:** Starting in 1943, the U.S. government eased the laws restricting Chinese immigration. Then, in 1965, the U.S. Congress passed the Immigration and Nationality Act, which made major changes in American immigration law. The 1965 law made it much easier for people from China (and other countries in Asia and elsewhere) to come to the United States.

The Land They Left

Starting in the 1800s, why did Chinese want to come to the United States? For centuries, China was one of the most advanced and powerful countries in the world. But by the 1800s, the Chinese government had grown weak, and European countries began to interfere in China's affairs more and more.

In the middle of the nineteenth century, Britain and France defeated China in two wars fought over the right to control trade with China. These wars left China even weaker. In some areas, different rebel groups began fighting against the Chinese government, and even against one another. This fighting led to the destruction of farms and towns. Another problem was that in some parts of China the population had grown very large, and it became difficult to grow enough food to feed everyone.

Chinese who lived along the coast knew about foreign lands because many foreign ships came to their port cities. Then, in 1848, gold was discovered in California. This was the start of the California Gold Rush. Ships brought the news to China, and many Chinese decided that California was the place to go. Chinese called California "Gold Mountain."

Working in the American West

Mining companies in California wanted the Chinese to come. There was a shortage of workers. The companies printed flyers in Chinese and sent them to China. At first, the Chinese worked as laborers for the mining companies. But then some of them went out on their own, and a few struck it rich. By the end of the 1850s, one out of every four miners in California was Chinese.

Mining companies were not the only American companies that welcomed the Chinese. Chinese workers were also needed to help build the first transcontinental railroad—that is, the first railroad to connect the eastern United States with the Pacific coast. Thousands of Chinese immigrants worked on this project.

Although most of the first Chinese immigrants worked in mining and railroad building, some went into other fields. The men who worked in mining needed lots of supplies and other services, and some Chinese immigrants quickly began catering to these needs. Washing clothes was considered a job for women, but there were very few women in California. So some industrious Chinese decided to open laundries and did very well. Some Chinese worked as carpenters building houses. Others became fishermen and fish sellers. Others opened restaurants and stores that sold food and equipment to miners.

Chinese immigrants also helped make California a major agricultural state. Many of the Chinese had been farmers in China and knew how to grow crops. They drained marshes. They created ways to irrigate fields. They grew all kinds of vegetables and fruits. Today California is one of the greatest fruit and vegetable growing centers in the world, and Chinese immigrants helped to make it so.

Some Chinese immigrants on the West Coast worked as doctors. They used Chinese herbal medicines to treat all types of illnesses. One of the most popular Chinese doctors was Ing Hay, who was known as "Doc" Hay. He was born in China in 1862 and came to the United States when he was nineteen. Many people in his family had studied traditional Chinese medicine. Ing Hay settled in

Ing Hay at age nineteen. After settling in Oregon, he became famous as the "China doctor" whose herbal remedies could treat illnesses and make people feel better.

Oregon in a town called John Day. There he became part-
ners with another Chinese immigrant, named Lung On.
First they opened a store. Then Ing Hay began practicing
medicine. He had about five hundred different herbs on his
shelves that he used to make medicines. Doc Hay became
famous for treating illnesses that other doctors couldn't
cure. Both Chinese and non-Chinese traveled for miles to
see the famous "China doctor."

A Society of Men

Most Chinese immigrants to the American West in the
nineteenth century were men. The work in mining and
railroad building was hard and at that time considered
suitable for men only. The cost of the trip was high. And
women were needed to look after families back in China.
In the early days of Chinese immigration to California,
there were more than a thousand Chinese men for every
Chinese woman. The early Chinese community on the
West Coast has been called a "bachelor society."

In the 1860s, a U.S. senator from California called these
male Chinese immigrants "sojourners." He and others
believed that the immigrants were not interested in staying
in the United States, just in making some money and then
returning to China. This belief led some U.S. politicians to
argue that Chinese immigrants should not be allowed to
become citizens.

But not every Chinese immigrant was a "sojourner."
Many did want to stay in the United States. Some brought
their wives over from China. By 1870, there were only

about twelve men for every woman among the almost 65,000 Chinese Americans living in the United States. Also by 1870, there were nearly four hundred Chinese-American children in California. Chinese immigrants were setting up families in their new country and planning to make the United States their permanent home.

Chinese immigrants at this time did not live only in California and other parts of the West. A Chinese neighborhood was established in New York City in the 1840s. New York City's Chinatown is still there today. A small number of Chinese also went to Boston, Philadelphia, and Baltimore. Some of the East Coast's early Chinese residents were sailors; others were cooks, merchants, doctors, and even cigar makers.

Anti-Chinese Actions

At first Chinese immigrants were welcomed to California and other parts of the West. But the welcome did not last. After a time, some American workers began to view the Chinese as competition for jobs. In some communities, groups of miners and railway workers tried to chase Chinese workers out of town. In San Francisco in 1877, an angry mob attacked the city's Chinatown for three nights in a row. They beat up immigrants and set fire to businesses. In 1885 in Tacoma, Washington, Chinese were forced to leave their homes, and their neighborhood was burned. A year later, rioters in Seattle burned down the Chinese part of town. In Oregon in 1887, a gang killed thirty-one Chinese miners. This incident became known as the Snake River Massacre.

Building the Transcontinental Railroad

One of the most remarkable things Chinese workers did in the United States in the nineteenth century was to help build the first railroad to run all the way across the country. Construction began in 1863, even though the United States was fighting the Civil War (1861–1865).

The railroad was built in two parts. The eastern part began in Omaha, Nebraska, and went west (rail lines already existed east of Nebraska). The Union Pacific Railroad company built this line. The western part started in Sacramento, California, and went east. This line was built by the Central Pacific Railroad company. The plan was for the two lines to meet in between.

Building the railroad was a huge project that required thousands of workers. The railroad companies—and especially the Central Pacific—found it hard to get enough people. Then someone suggested using Chinese workers. At first, some believed the Chinese were too weak for such hard labor. They soon learned that the Chinese could work as hard as anyone. The president of the Central Pacific even said that the Chinese were "much more reliable" than other workers. Soon the owners of the Central Pacific sent people to China to hire workers. The transcontinental railroad was finished in 1869. By then 17,000 laborers had worked on the western section; 15,000 of them were Chinese.

A total of 15,000 Chinese laborers worked on the western section of the first transcontinental railroad, cutting through California's rugged Sierra Nevada mountains.

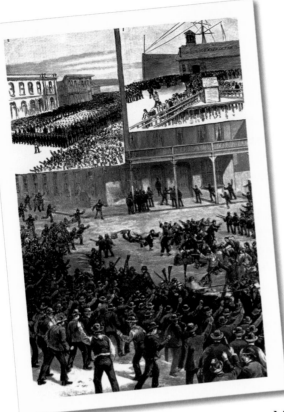

Chinese in Seattle were attacked and their neighborhood was burned down in 1886, as shown in this newspaper illustration from that time.

Many politicians in the West won votes by promising to solve the "Chinese question." Labor unions supported laws that barred Chinese immigrants from working in certain jobs, for example, in mining. By 1910, there were no Chinese miners in California, Montana, Arizona, or Colorado. The anti-Chinese labor laws caused many Chinese to move out of the West. Some went to Midwest cities like Chicago and St. Louis. It was at this time that some U.S. cities got their first Chinatowns.

Other laws were passed that made life difficult for the Chinese. In California, a law was passed that required a certain amount of space for each person living in a house. It was known as the cubic air law. It was aimed at crowded Chinese boardinghouses. Some places required a business-person to pay a large fee in order to be allowed to open a laundry. A San Francisco law required that any man who went to jail had to have his hair cut to an inch (2.5 centimeters) in length; this law also was aimed at Chinese immigrants, since at that time Chinese men wore a long braid down their back called a queue. In many states at the beginning of the twentieth century, it was a crime for Chinese and other nonwhite people to marry a white person. In 1913, California passed a law that prohibited Chinese (and other Asian) immigrants from owning land.

Fighting Back

Chinese Americans fought back against many of the anti-Chinese laws. One who fought back was a Chinese immigrant named Ho Ah Kow. He went to jail in San Francisco for breaking the cubic air law. While he was in jail, his queue was cut off. Ho sued, and a judge agreed his rights had been violated. The law on cutting hair was struck down, and Ho was awarded $10,000. This case was important in U.S. history because the court concluded that even residents who were not citizens of the United

A number of early Chinese immigrants went into the laundry business. This illustration shows a laundry in California in the 1850s.

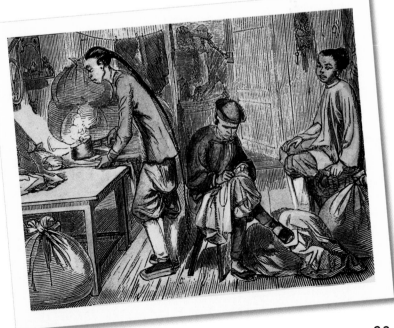

States still were entitled to certain rights that had to be protected under the U.S. Constitution.

Another important court case had to do with laws that made it difficult for Chinese to run laundries. In San Francisco, a law was passed in 1880 that said all laundries had to be in stone or brick buildings. Laundries in wooden buildings could be acceptable, too, but only with the approval of the board of supervisors. In San Francisco in the 1880s, more than two hundred laundries in wooden buildings were owned by Chinese immigrants, and all were refused approval by the board of supervisors to continue operating. There were eighty laundries not owned by Chinese immigrants that were in wooden buildings, and of these, all but one received approval to continue operating. One of the Chinese-American laundry owners, named Yick Wo, was arrested and jailed for continuing to operate his laundry without approval. In 1886, the U.S. Supreme Court ruled that Yick Wo had to be set free. The justices concluded that the way the San Francisco law was administered amounted to **discrimination** against Chinese immigrants; therefore, what the board of supervisors had done violated the equal protection of the law that all people in the United States are entitled to under the U.S. Constitution.

Still another major U.S. Supreme Court decision was handed down in the case of Chinese American Wong Kim Ark. His parents were immigrants from China, but he was born in the United States (in San Francisco) in 1873. In 1894, he decided to visit China. When he returned to California the next year, he was told that he could not enter the United States because U.S. law at that time barred almost all immigrants from China. Wong Kim Ark hired a lawyer. He argued that he was not an immigrant but an American citizen coming back to his homeland. In an 1898 decision, the U.S. Supreme Court agreed. The Court concluded that the U.S. Constitution provides that virtually all people born in the United States are automatically citizens of the United States—and this has been the law of the land ever since.

Chinese Exclusion

Some Americans' anti-Chinese **prejudices** led to legislation to keep Chinese immigrants from coming to the United States. In 1882, the U.S. Congress passed a law called the Chinese Exclusion Act. It said that for the next ten years no Chinese workers could enter the United States, and it also said that Chinese immigrants already in the United States could not become citizens. (The law did, however, still allow Chinese merchants and students to come to the United States.) An even tougher law, the Geary

Ah Bing and Poison Jim

Bing cherries, the most popular cherries in the United States, got their name from a Chinese immigrant farmer who lived in the West. His name was Ah Bing. Around 1855 he went to work for a man in Oregon who was in the orchard business. While working at the orchard, Ah Bing cultivated the cherry that now bears his name.

Another Chinese immigrant farmer was known as Poison Jim. While walking around the Salinas Valley in California sometime in the late 1850s, he saw wild mustard plants growing like weeds. Mustard was popular in China, so he knew what the plants were. The local farmers didn't want the mustard plants, so they let Jim take them. He hired some Chinese workers to remove the seeds from the plants and make them into mustard, which he started selling. Then, one year, the mustard crop in Europe didn't grow. A French businessman came to California and paid Poison Jim $35,000 for his mustard seed. Jim became rich, and mustard became a major California product.

Chinatowns

A number of U.S. cities have a neighborhood called Chinatown. These are areas where the population is mostly Chinese American. Today, Chinatowns are often tourist attractions. Visitors come to shop in open-air markets, jewelry stores, and gift shops. They eat in Chinese restaurants and tea houses.

Most Chinatowns originally developed as places where Chinese immigrants could feel more at home among people who shared their language and customs. The term *Chinatown* was being used in San Francisco as early as the 1850s. As anti-Chinese laws were passed and Chinese immigrants were sometimes physically harmed, Chinatowns also became safe havens. In these neighborhoods, Chinese Americans could feel more secure. Residents of Chinatowns created their own organizations. They founded self-help groups and trade associations. They established their own newspapers. They built shrines and temples to practice their religions (Confucianism, Buddhism, and Taoism were the major religions in China). In San Francisco in 1900, Chinese-American organizations got together and opened their own hospital.

The buildings are some of the most interesting things about Chinatowns. Often the architecture is a blend of Western and Chinese styles. Sometimes the buildings have carved columns with Chinese inscriptions on them. Buildings are often painted in bright colors like red, green, and gold.

Act, was passed in 1892. It extended the ban on Chinese immigration for another ten years. The Chinese Exclusion Act was extended again in 1902, and then, in 1904, Congress made the ban on Chinese immigration permanent.

For more than sixty years after the passage of the first exclusion act of 1882, hardly any Chinese immigrants entered the United States. The Chinese-American population began to shrink. In 1910, there were only about 70,000 Chinese Americans in the United States. In 1920, there were about 60,000.

Welcome Again

The government began to ease the restrictions on Chinese immigration in the 1940s. In 1937, Japan invaded China. By 1939, most of the world was involved in fighting World War II. The United States entered the war

These Chinese Americans (their visors pushed up for the photo) worked as welders at a U.S. government shipyard during World War II, helping to build warships.

in December 1941 when Japanese planes attacked the U.S. Navy base at Pearl Harbor in Hawaii. Now, China and the United States were allies. People in the United States started to view the Chinese people as brave fighters against Japanese aggression. In December 1943, after President Franklin D. Roosevelt sent a letter to Congress saying that it was time to "correct a historic mistake," Congress repealed the Chinese Exclusion Act. Chinese immigrants again became eligible for U.S. citizenship, and Chinese could again immigrate to the United States, although the number allowed initially was quite small: only 105 people a year. But the repeal of the Chinese Exclusion Act was just the beginning. Later, the number of immigrants allowed to enter would grow.

One result of the United States' entering World War II was a shortage of American workers. U.S. factories were operating around the clock making weapons and other things needed for the war. But millions of men who had been factory workers went into the army and navy. This

Chinese Communist leader Mao Zedong (*in dark coat*) rides into Beijing in triumph in 1949, after Communist forces captured the city.

opened up job opportunities for Chinese Americans and other minority groups.

One of the biggest changes involved Chinese-American women. Before the war, most Chinese-American women stayed home and took care of their families. Now they began going to work in factories and on military bases. They got to meet people of other backgrounds. They had their own money to spend. They were also proud to show that they could do a job just as well as any American man. After the war, many of these women kept on working. Some of them went on to higher education. In many ways, World War II was a liberating experience for a number of Chinese-American women.

Many Chinese-American men worked in factories that made war supplies, and almost one out of every four Chinese-American men served in the military. These men often found that when they put on a uniform, white Americans were less likely to feel prejudice toward them. Many white American soldiers came to think highly of their Chinese-American comrades.

After World War II, China was in a civil war. The Communists won and took control of the Chinese government in 1949. The U.S. government opposed the spread of Communism, and China became an enemy of the United States. (Relations between the United States and China did not begin to improve until the early 1970s.) Many Chinese on the losing side of the civil war decided to leave China rather than live under Communism. Some managed to enter the United States by claiming that they were the children of Chinese who were American citizens. Others had been high-level officials in China who feared they would be treated harshly by the new Communist government. They were admitted to the United States as **refugees**. Some Chinese students in the United States who had intended to return to China now didn't want to leave and were allowed to stay. The stage was set for a new era in Chinese immigration to the United States.

The New York City neighborhood of Flushing is one of several in the city with large Chinese-American populations.

CHAPTER THREE

THE NEW IMMIGRANTS

In the early days of Chinese immigration, the United States needed Chinese workers for jobs like mining and railroad building. In the years after World War II, the United States wanted a different type of worker—college-educated professionals. The United States wanted engineers and scientists. So immigration laws were changed to make it easier for people with such skills to enter the United States. Family reunification—that is, making it easier for residents of the United States to bring family members from other countries to join them—also became a goal of immigration policy at this time. The Immigration and Nationality Act of 1952 established these two preferences in the granting of **immigrant visas**.

Thirteen years later, the Immigration and Nationality Act of 1965 made even greater changes to U.S. immigration law. In general, it allowed a larger number of immigrants to enter the United States each year, including 170,000 from the Eastern Hemisphere (the part of the world that includes Asia, Africa, and Europe). Of this total, up to 20,000 people could come from any one country, including China. (Initially, the maximum for China included Taiwan and Hong Kong, but in the 1970s, these areas were given separate maximums.) Family reunification and occupational skills were the main criteria for granting immigrant visas.

Under another provision of the 1965 act, the actual number of immigrants from a single country could turn out to be more than 20,000 a year. That's because the spouses, children, and parents of U.S. citizens could immigrate to the United States without being counted toward the 20,000 limit.

In 1960 the Chinese-American population in the United States was about 237,000. By 1970, it had almost doubled. The Chinese-American population also began to spread out, seeking economic opportunities in new areas. California still had the most Chinese Americans, but New York State was second. There were also large numbers of Chinese Americans in Hawaii, Illinois, Massachusetts, New Jersey, Washington, and Texas.

Most of the Chinese immigrants in the first decade or so after the 1965 act went into effect came from Taiwan and Hong Kong. The mainland Chinese government was not allowing immigration to the United States (or to most other

A Chinese-American graduate student enjoys graduation day at Harvard University.

countries) at that time. The Chinese government's policy on immigration began to change in the late 1970s, and in recent decades, immigration from the mainland, as well as continuing immigration from Taiwan and Hong Kong, has been a major factor in the growth of the Chinese-American population. This population was more than 800,000 by 1980. It had doubled to more than 1.6 million by 1990. It increased significantly again and had reached almost 2.6 million by the year 2000.

Coming to Study—and to Stay

By the late twentieth century, many young Chinese were coming to the United States to study at American universities—and often to stay permanently afterward. This was true of students both from the mainland and from Taiwan.

Many of the students followed the same path. They would go to graduate school on **temporary visas** and study science, engineering, or medicine. After finishing school, they would find a job in the United States. There, they would ask their employer to sponsor them for permanent residence based upon their occupational skills.

One area that attracted educated Chinese immigrants was the region of California south of San Francisco known as Silicon Valley. This is where many large computer and technology firms are located. Some people have compared the Chinese immigration to Silicon Valley to the original Gold Rush, which had attracted so many Chinese immigrants in the 1850s. This time, however, it was not gold that the immigrants were looking for but silicon, as in silicon computer chips.

Arrival of the Fujianese

Not all recent Chinese immigrants have been well-educated professionals. Since the late 1970s, many other Chinese have come to the United States as well, in part because the Chinese government changed its policy toward immigration and in part because of major economic changes occurring in China. In 1978, China's government began an ambitious economic development program. It allowed Western companies to come to China to do business and to help China's modernization. The government changed its agricultural policy and allowed farmers to sell their products on the open market. It encouraged small businesses to start up. It welcomed foreign trade and allowed students to go to U.S. universities. It began to permit most Chinese citizens who wanted to become immigrants to leave China and go to other countries.

Also beginning in the late 1970s, the Chinese government set up special economic development areas on the coast of southern China. Over time, these areas became wealthier, and their cities grew rapidly. For example, the population of the southern coastal city of Guangzhou (formerly Canton) went from about 3 million in 1990 to more than 7 million in 2000. Chinese who lived in nearby rural areas decided to move to these coastal cities in order to find jobs.

Soon the cities began to be overcrowded. As a result, many Chinese looking for more economic opportunity decided to do what Chinese had done a hundred years before: go to the United States. Many of these new Chinese immigrants were from the province of Fujian. People from this region are known as Fujianese.

Many of the Fujianese did not have relatives in the United States or professional skills. They found it difficult to get permission to enter the United States. Many of them have entered without permission, as undocumented immigrants. Although it is difficult to know how many undocumented immigrants have come to the United States from China, the U.S. government estimated that by 2007 the figure was 290,000.

Tiananmen Square

In China in 1989, protests by students and others demanding political reforms began. The largest demonstrations took place in Beijing, the capital, in an area called Tiananmen Square. In early June, the Chinese government sent in tanks and troops to break up the protests. Many demonstrators were wounded or killed. After that, U.S. president George H. W. Bush signed a special order. It allowed any Chinese citizens who were in the United States on or after June 5, 1989, to stay in the country if they wished. Then, in 1992, the U.S. Congress passed the Chinese Student Protection Act. This law allowed all mainland Chinese students who were studying in the United States at the time that the Tiananmen Square protests were broken up to become permanent U.S. residents if they wished.

A lone protestor tries to face down tanks heading to break up the Tiananmen Square demonstrations.

Many of these new immigrants have been smuggled into the United States on ships. The smugglers arranging their transportation became known as **snakeheads**. This is because the route an undocumented immigrant takes often can have many curves, like the body of a snake. A snakehead often charges an immigrant a lot of money, sometimes as much as $60,000. Fujianese farmers often do not have that kind of money. Many borrow from family and friends, hoping they can make enough money in the United States to pay back the debt. Also, once they have a job in the United States, many are able to send money back home to help their families.

But hiring a snakehead can be dangerous. In 1993 a ship called the *Golden Venture*, carrying 286 Chinese, ran aground on a sandbar near New York City. Ten of the would-be immigrants died, and many more were injured as they tried to get to shore. The police put the rest in jail. Eventually, some of them were sent back to China. Some were allowed to remain in the United States.

Rescuers try to get people off the grounded ship *Golden Venture*, which was carrying hundreds of undocumented Chinese immigrants to New York.

Jerry Yang, Computer Pioneer

Jerry Yang is one of the most successful innovators and business leaders in the computer industry. In the mid–1990s, he and his partner, David Filo, created the Internet portal and search engine Yahoo! Although in 2008 the company's stock decreased in value and Yang stepped down as chief executive officer, the Yahoo! service was being used by almost 500 million people around the world. Yang himself was said to be worth more than $2 billion.

Yang was born in Taiwan in 1968. He moved to California with his family when he was ten. After high school he went to Stanford University, where he became friends with David Filo. When Jerry and David were at Stanford, the World Wide Web was just getting started. The two friends decided to create a list of their favorite websites. It was called *David and Jerry's Guide to the World Wide Web*. They sent the list to other computer users, who found it very useful. Soon the list got very long. Jerry and David decided that they had to break it into sections. They also created hyperlinks to help people connect to other websites. Eventually, so many people were using Jerry's website that the computers at Stanford crashed. Jerry and David had to move off campus and set up their own offices. That was the beginning of Yahoo!

Another way undocumented Chinese immigrants have been able to enter the United States is by buying fake papers. This can also be extremely expensive.

The Fujianese reaching the United States have often been under pressure to repay their debts. Often the money they borrow from friends and family is just a "down payment" on the full cost of the trip. It's not unusual for the rest of the money to be borrowed either from the snakeheads or from Chinese gangsters. Those having trouble making payments have sometimes been the victims of violence. To make money, some immigrants have taken low-paying jobs and worked very long hours, often on construction sites, in restaurants, or in sweatshops. Their employers often treat these workers badly, knowing that the workers are unlikely to go to the authorities to complain—if their undocumented status is discovered, they can be forced to leave the United States.

Even though they have difficult lives and earn very little, many of the immigrants still find it worthwhile to come to the United States. One immigrant explained to a researcher that it would take a worker in China fifteen years to earn what he could make in the United States in one.

Many of the Fujianese arriving in the United States do not speak English. So they live in Chinatowns, where they can be with other Chinese immigrants who speak their native language. The populations of Chinatowns have grown quickly. Living conditions for many of the immigrants can be crowded and uncomfortable.

Moving Out of Chinatown

Many better-educated and more **affluent** Chinese Americans have decided to seek better living conditions outside the traditional Chinatowns. For example, in New York City in the 1970s, Chinese Americans began moving into a suburban-like middle-class area called Flushing. Initially, most of the Chinese who moved there were from Hong Kong or Taiwan. Eventually, Chinese from mainland China followed them to Flushing and nearby neighborhoods. Today, the Flushing area has a large Chinese-American community (and also sizable communities of other Asian Americans). Many stores, schools, and businesses of all kinds advertise in Chinese and provide goods and services that meet the needs and preferences of Chinese Americans.

In other parts of the United States, Chinese Americans have moved into suburbs outside major cities. For example, in the 1990s the Chinese-American population of the city

Return of the Sea Turtles

As China's economy has boomed and economic opportunities in China have increased, some Chinese immigrants in the United States have decided to go back. These people are known in China as "**sea turtles**." That's because the Chinese phrase for sea turtle is *hai gui*. That sounds like *haiwai guilai*, which means "returned from overseas."

The returnees—educated at American universities—have skills that are needed in China. They speak both English and Chinese, and they understand both Western and Chinese ways.

Some sea turtles find themselves torn between East and West. After spending so much time in the United States, they miss things like American television and American food.

Some of them become very pro-China. Sometimes this happens because they had bad experiences in the United States. For example, some speak English with an accent and felt that, because of this, they could never get ahead in the United States. Others found anti-Chinese prejudice in the United States. Some felt that many Americans did not know—or care to know—much about China.

of Los Angeles actually went down. But the Chinese-American population of the suburbs around Los Angeles went up by more than 34 percent. In the 1980s, many Taiwanese immigrants began to settle in Fremont, California, outside San Francisco. Taiwanese Americans started businesses of all kinds in Fremont and set up schools to teach Chinese to their children. By the mid–1990s, there were about 100 high-tech firms in the Fremont area that either had been started by Taiwanese Americans or were branches of companies in Taiwan.

Going Back to China

By the 1990s and early twenty-first century, the economic changes begun in China in the late 1970s had produced dramatic results. China's economy was the fastest growing in the world, and China had become the world's biggest manufacturer.

Trade between the United States and China greatly increased.

Job opportunities in China's modern cities, such as Beijing (*shown here*), are luring some Chinese immigrants back to their native country.

Chinese Americans who could speak Chinese and who understood Chinese customs were in a good position to be go-betweens between China and the United States. U.S. employment agencies began looking for Chinese Americans to help U.S. companies operate in and do business with China. Some U.S.-educated Chinese returned to China to advise the government on how to make economic reforms. Some Chinese immigrants, seeing new economic opportunities in China, have gone back to China to stay.

Two Chinese-American high school students conduct an experiment as part of a research project.

CHAPTER FOUR

MAKING A NEW LIFE

I n the late 1960s, when Chinese immigrants started coming to the United States in large numbers, it was a time of great change in the United States. Minority groups were actively working against prejudice and discrimination and asking for full equality. Many were inspired by the civil rights movement, which had been fighting for equal rights for African Americans.

Fighting for Their Rights

Chinese Americans had faced discrimination since they first came to California more than a century earlier. In the 1960s, one of the first Chinese-American equal rights organizations formed was the Asian American Political Alliance, or AAPA, founded in the San Francisco area in 1968. Another organization, Asian Americans for Action, was founded in New York City the same year.

A group called Asian Americans for Equality, or AAFE, was founded in 1974. It also began in New York City, where a high-rise development called Confucius Plaza was being built. Even though the construction site was right in the middle of Chinatown, the builder would not hire Chinese workers. Protesters demonstrated at the construction site. After six months the builder gave in and agreed to hire minority workers. Today AAFE continues to fight for the rights of Chinese and other Asian Americans.

The oldest Chinese-American advocacy organization is the Chinese Consolidated Benevolent Association. It was established in San Francisco in the 1850s. Then it was known as the Six Companies. Today it has branches in many cities.

Besides forming organizations to work for equal rights, Chinese and other Asian Americans sought recognition in another way. In the late 1960s, Asian-American students asked universities to set up departments that would teach Asian-American studies. The first one to do so was San Francisco State College, which is now called San Francisco State University. Today, more than two dozen U.S. universities have such departments.

The ABCs

Today about 30 percent of Chinese Americans were born in the United States. The term *American-born Chinese* is

A Chinese-American boy in
San Francisco looks through family
photographs with his grandparents.

sometimes abbreviated as ABC. The members of this
group (ABCs) often face special challenges because they
are divided between two cultures.

Some of the challenges for American-born Chinese
come from the closeness of traditional Chinese families.
A Chinese name shows one way the family is so important.

In nearly all Western countries, the given name comes first, and the family name comes last. In a Chinese name the family name comes first. In the name Mao Zedong, for example, Mao is the family name. The Chinese tradition of putting the family name first suggests that the family comes first. A Chinese family is traditionally a place where family members can feel secure. It is common for an **extended family** to live in the same household—not just parents and their children but grandparents and other family members as well. The Chinese family also tends to have a strong sense of who is an "insider" and who is an "outsider" (that is, someone outside the family). Chinese immigrant parents sometimes warn their children against "outsiders." If a child needs help, that child is expected to get it from the family. The child is not expected to get it from a teacher or other person outside the family.

A popular Chinese expression is *ting hua*. These are words of advice given to children. The expression means that children should always listen to adults and do as they are told. Chinese children are not encouraged to speak up and explain what they want. In traditional Chinese families, they are told to get along and not make a fuss. Chinese-American parents are often surprised at how American children complain and demand things. This Chinese attitude spills over into school. In Chinese schools children are expected to listen. In American schools they are expected to raise their hands and ask questions.

Chinese-American children born in the United States do not always feel as suspicious of "outsiders" as their

One Person's Story: "Embracing the 'Twinkie'"

In June 2008, a twenty-three-year-old Chinese American named Christy Wong wrote an essay published online by the *Chicago Tribune* newspaper entitled "Being Chinese American and Embracing the 'Twinkie.'" (*Twinkie* is a slang term for assimilated young Chinese Americans, who are said to be yellow on the outside but white on the inside.) In the essay, Wong talked about her assimilation into American life:

"I am a Twinkie, perhaps a different type of Twinkie. . . . At a young age, I thought of myself as purely American, in fact, much more American than Chinese. . . . My parents didn't teach us Chinese. Neither did they make us attend Chinese school. . . .

"Throughout elementary school to the beginning of my high school years, my closest friends were white. By junior year, I had more Asian-American friends. I felt like I could blend easily into both groups, but I felt more comfortable among my white friends.

"In college, culture shock ensued. I attended Taylor University in a predominately white and rural Indiana community. For the first time, I felt like a minority."

When Christy was a junior in college, she went to Poland with some other students from the university. They were there to teach English to high school students.

"I identified myself as American, but that wasn't how the Poles perceived me. [T]hey said I didn't look like the 'typical' American. . . . It was the first time I felt totally aware of my Chinese heritage."

She also took a trip to China. There she found that the people considered her Chinese, not American. They couldn't understand why she couldn't speak Chinese. Christy decided she would study the language.

"As I've grown older and spent more time with my Asian-American friends, I have gained a greater appreciation for my Chinese background. I am learning how to integrate some Chinese values and beliefs into my American culture in order to find a balance between the two."

parents. They are more influenced by American culture, and they tend not to be as willing to be obedient and undemanding. For this and other reasons, there is often tension between parents and children.

Chinese-American children born in the United States can feel divided between two cultures. Their parents encourage traditional Chinese ways. But the children watch American television, go to American schools, and have non-Chinese friends. Some of these children experience "identity confusion." Are they Chinese? Are they American? Of course, they are both. But it's not always easy to be bicultural.

At the same time that they are adopting American ways, Chinese-American children may still find anti-Chinese prejudice among their classmates. Other children in school sometimes tease Chinese-American children because they look different, tease them about their names, or even bully them or beat them up. Some young Chinese Americans react by avoiding other children and staying with Chinese friends. Some go the other way. They work extra hard to make non-Chinese friends. And some try to have it both ways and live in both worlds.

Those young Chinese Americans who prefer to socialize with other Chinese

One Person's Story: Zhen (Tony) Wu

Zhen (Tony) Wu is a network support specialist for the New York City Department of Education and a former assistant principal at Public School 105 in Brooklyn, New York. P.S. 105 is a school with a mostly Chinese-American enrollment.

Tony's mother was born in San Jose, California, in 1928 to Chinese immigrant parents. Then, when she was seven, "grandpa, having a small fortune and being nostalgic, decided to move the family back to his hometown, Doumen," which is in Guangdong Province, China, near Hong Kong. The family moved to the offshore island of Macau during World War II and returned to Doumen after Japan surrendered and the war ended in 1945.

However, the victory over the Japanese did not bring the family many happy years, Tony says. "In 1949, the Communists took over China, and my grandpa was executed by the government because he protested the confiscation [government takeover] of his property. Many members of the family were stoned to death by . . . villagers, who later divided among themselves the land and houses owned by my grandpa. My mother was a college student in Canton [now Guangzhou, the capital city of Guangdong Province] and escaped the massacres in China's rural areas that year."

In 1955, Tony's parents got married, and he was born in Guangzhou in 1958. Tony explains, "I graduated from high school in 1975 and was sent to a government-owned tea plantation to be 're-edu-

Tony Wu at his
desk when he
was an assis-
tant principal
at a New York
City elementary
school.

cated,' which was one of [the government's] strategies [under Communist leader Mao Zedong] to control restless students. My parents were sent to rural areas at an earlier time for the same purpose."

Following Mao's death and some liberalization of Chinese government policies, Tony returned to Guangzhou in 1978 and went to college for his bachelor's and master's degrees. In 1988, with the assistance of the American Consulate at Guangzhou, his mother was able to return to the United States, and he joined her in 1991. By this time, he had married. "My daughter, Helen, was born in China and my son, Harry, was born in New York. My wife, Jenny, joined me in 1996 and graduated from New York University. She is a social worker. My father [who came to the United States in 1994] and mother are both living in Brooklyn, enjoying their peaceful life."

Tony describes this way why he thinks many Chinese-American students do so well in school: "There is something in the Chinese culture and this 'something' can be described as follows in my opinion. Education has been considered the key to success throughout China's entire history since Confucius [the fifth-century B.C.E. Chinese philosopher]. There is a famous saying that almost every Chinese parent knows: 'Of all the ways to prepare for a successful career, all is inferior to education.' Teachers receive high respect from all walks of life even when they make very little for a living."

To be hardworking, says Tony, is also something the Chinese consider an "important virtue. Another saying that has been passed from generation to generation is that you can only be better than the others if you work harder than the others. Being lazy or good for nothing would be looked down upon in all Chinese societies [around] the world."

Responsibility for family (including the extended family) "is expected for Chinese youngsters. Since education is considered the best way to prepare for a good career and one can only fulfill his or her responsibility to family financially by having a good career, it is natural that the Chinese work very hard in school and do their best to get into a prestigious college."

Many Chinese-American students work
very hard to do well in school.

Americans sometimes make fun of the ones who don't. They have insulting slang expressions for their more Americanized peers—such as "Twinkie" or "banana" (meaning yellow on the outside but white on the inside). Being very Americanized is a choice that many young Chinese Americans make. (For some who live in areas where there are not many other Chinese Americans, there may not really be another option.) It is not uncommon for U.S.-born Chinese Americans today to marry someone who is not Chinese.

Success in School

Since Chinese families tend to value education so highly and encourage their children to spend a lot of time on homework and studying, it is quite common for Chinese-American students to do well in school. Many graduate from high school with excellent academic records and are able to attend top colleges and universities.

Of course, not all Chinese-American students do well in school. Every group of people includes a wide range of individuals with varying talents, abilities, and experiences. Some parents (including low-income families struggling to earn a living) may, for example, be too busy working to oversee or encourage their children's attention to school-work. Like children and teens of all ethnic backgrounds, some Chinese-American young people struggle in and even drop out of school, use illegal drugs, join gangs, or in other ways do not fit the **stereotype** that all Chinese-American students are well-behaved high achievers.

One of the most successful animated films
of 2008 featured a panda kung fu enthusiast.
The Chinese martial art has become extremely
popular in the United States.

CHAPTER FIVE

CHANGING THE AMERICAN CULTURE

Chinese Americans have made their mark in American business, government, science, the arts and entertainment, and many other fields. And aspects of Chinese culture have become part of the American mainstream, although perhaps in modified form.

The part of Chinese culture that is probably best known to many Americans is Chinese food. Surveys show that Chinese food is one of the top three favorite ethnic foods in the United States. (The others are Italian food and Mexican food.) There are more than 40,000 Chinese restaurants in the United States. In some ways the food is different from the food in China. Some ingredients are different, and recipes have been adapted for American tastes.

Chinese Restaurants: A Long History

Chinese restaurants began with the early Chinese immigrants in California. In 1850 a reporter for the *New York Tribune* was telling his readers that Chinese immigrants had opened restaurants in San Jose, California. He said that one reason these restaurants were popular was that they gave customers a lot to eat.

For many years, most Chinese restaurants served Cantonese food—food that was based on the cooking in the region of China around the city of Canton (now Guangzhou). More recently, however, Chinese food based on the cooking in other parts of China has become popular. Today, Americans can enjoy Chinese restaurants that specialize in food from Hunan, Hong Kong, Shanghai, Taiwan, Sichuan, and other areas.

The Chinese Laundry

Next to restaurants, laundries are probably the most-often-seen type of Chinese American–owned businesses in the United States. Like Chinese restaurants, Chinese laundries began with the early Chinese immigrants in California. In 1851, a Chinese immigrant in San Francisco named Wah Lee opened a laundry. By 1870, more than 1,300 Chinese were working in the laundry business just in San Francisco. By 1880 there were more than 2,000 such workers. In 1900, about one out of every five Chinese men in San Francisco worked in a laundry. Chinese immigrants soon began to open laundries in other U.S. cities. In 1888, there were about 2,000 Chinese laundries in New York City.

As anti-Chinese laws in California and other parts of the West barred Chinese immigrants from working in mines, many Chinese men who were shut out from other jobs turned to the laundry business. Not many other American men were interested in going into the business because the work was so hard. Today, Chinese American–owned laundries are still common in many American cities and towns.

Martial Arts and Movies

In 2008, an American animated movie was released called *Kung Fu Panda*. A box office hit, the movie tells the story of a panda named Po who lives in China. He loves the Chinese martial art of kung fu and wants to become a kung fu master. Po takes lessons from the Furious Five. They are Tigress, Crane, Mantis, Viper, and Monkey. They are led by Master Shifu. It becomes Po's task, along with his new friends, to defeat the evil snow leopard Tai Lung.

Kung fu began to catch on in the United States in the early 1970s. An award-winning television series entitled *Kung Fu* first aired in 1972. In the year after *Kung Fu* first went on TV, the martial arts expert Bruce Lee released a movie called *Enter the Dragon*. This was the first American-made martial arts feature film. It made kung fu movies extremely popular. *Enter the Dragon* started a trend that continues today.

Bruce Lee's original name was Lee Jun Fan. He was born in San Francisco in 1940. His immigrant parents went back to Hong Kong when he was still a baby. At twelve he began to study Chinese martial arts. When Lee got in trouble with

the police, his parents sent him to the United States.
In 1966 he got a part in a television series called *The Green Hornet*. Then Lee returned to Hong Kong and began making kung fu movies that were big hits. Hollywood moviemakers invited him to come back to California. They made him the star of *Enter the Dragon*, which was a huge success. Sadly, Bruce Lee died from swelling of the brain in 1973, just before the movie came out.

Bruce Lee's influence has lasted. More recently, Jackie Chan followed in his footsteps. Jackie Chan's original name was Chan Kong-sang. He was born in Hong Kong. When he grew up, he pursued a career in movies. Chan realized that he could never be another Bruce Lee. He decided to try something new. He mixed adventure with comedy. His hit films helped make kung fu popular all over the world.

The movies of Bruce Lee and Jackie Chan have shown Americans one side of Chinese culture. Other films have shown other sides. In 1998, the Disney Studio released *Mulan*. This animated movie, based on an old Chinese folktale, tells the story of a Chinese girl who disguises herself as a man and takes her father's place in the army. Another very successful movie was *Crouching Tiger, Hidden Dragon*. It came out in 2000. This live-action movie used fantastic special effects. Warriors fight with swords while floating in the air, skimming over rooftops and trees.

Other Chinese Arts

Another ancient Chinese practice that has become popular in the United States is **acupuncture**. Acupuncture is a

Many American health professionals now use acupuncture with their patients.

way of deadening pain or of changing certain body conditions. It is done by sticking fine needles into the skin. The practice of acupuncture is very old. One Chinese book on acupuncture dates from about 100 B.C.E. Acupuncture was practiced in the United States in the 1800s, but it did not become well-known until the 1970s.

A Chinese art that has been catching on in the United States even more recently is **feng shui**. It is the art of arranging objects to create harmony and balance. The words *feng shui* mean "wind and water"—good winds and water traditionally have been associated with good harvests and health. The goal of feng shui is to achieve the best balance of all the forces that are believed to exist in a given space and to affect people's health and happiness. A place with the right combination of forces is supposed to have good feng shui. If objects in the home are put into the best position, the result is greater harmony.

Amy Tan

Amy Tan's first novel, *The Joy Luck Club*, was published in 1989. Praised by reviewers, it was on best-seller lists for months, and a hit movie based on the book came out in 1993. The book tells the story of four women who become friends. They create a club called the Joy Luck Club. They were all born in China and came to the United States. They also all have daughters, and they want their daughters to understand their pasts. The daughters are trying to understand and to appreciate their mothers' sacrifices. The families experience both conflict and love.

Chinese American Amy Tan based *The Joy Luck Club* on her own experiences. She was born in California to Chinese immigrant parents. Tan has said that she started writing the book for her mother. Her relationship with her mother was like that of many Chinese-American children who feel caught between the Chinese culture of their parents and the American culture in which they live.

Since *The Joy Luck Club*, Amy Tan has written several other novels. All of them were bestsellers.

Author Amy Tan at her home in New York City.

Famous Chinese Americans

Chinese Americans have made outstanding contributions and achieved success in many fields. For example, the movie *Crouching Tiger, Hidden Dragon* was directed by the Chinese-American filmmaker Ang Lee. Ang Lee was born in Taiwan in 1954. He came to the United States in 1979 to study theater and film production. His first hit movie was *The Wedding Banquet* in 1993. After that, he went on to make such highly praised movies as *Eat Drink Man Woman,*

The Ice Storm, Sense and Sensibility, Ride with the Devil, Hulk, and *Brokeback Mountain*, for which Ang Lee won the 2005 Academy Award for best director.

Lucy Liu is another Chinese American who has been successful in films and on television. She was born in New York City in 1968 to immigrant parents. Liu got the lead in a college play and decided to pursue acting. In 2000 she had two big movie successes. She starred in *Shanghai Noon* with Jackie Chan, and she was one of the leads in *Charlie's Angels*. In 2008, she was the voice of the Viper in *Kung Fu Panda*.

When journalist Connie Chung became the co-anchor of the *CBS Evening News* in 1993, she was the first Chinese American to become a nightly news anchor at a major television network. Today Chinese-American women journalists are regularly seen on news broadcasts across the United States. Chung's full name is Constance Yu-hwa Chung. She was born outside Washington, D.C., to Chinese immigrant parents. Her father was a Nationalist diplomat, and the family fled to the United States during the Chinese civil war in the 1940s.

Renowned Chinese-American architect I. M. Pei was born in Canton (now Guangzhou), China, in 1917. He first came to the United States at the age of seventeen to study architecture. He opened his own architecture firm in 1955. His buildings became famous for their simple and stylish designs, and Pei has won many major architecture awards. Perhaps his most famous design is the glass and steel pyramid in a courtyard of the Louvre Museum in Paris, France.

The Rock and Roll Hall of Fame and Museum in Cleveland, Ohio, was designed by Chinese-American architect I. M. Pei.

When Pei designed the Rock and Roll Hall of Fame and Museum in Cleveland, Ohio, he also incorporated a pyramid.

The Vietnam Veterans Memorial in Washington, D.C., is another structure designed by a Chinese American. It is a sloping V-shaped wall made of black granite. On it are the names of more than 58,000 Americans killed or missing during the Vietnam War of the 1960s and 1970s. The memorial was designed by Maya Lin when she was still in college. She was born in Ohio in 1959. Her parents were immigrants from China. While she was at Yale University, a national contest was held to find the best design for a memorial to honor Americans who had served in the Vietnam War. Everyone was surprised when the contest was won by someone who was only twenty-one years old.

One of the most famous cello players in the world is Yo-Yo Ma. He was born in 1955 to Chinese parents living in Paris. His family moved to New York when he was very young, and that was where he grew up. He studied cello at the famous Juilliard School in New York. He has performed with nearly all of the great orchestras in the world.

Vera Wang is perhaps the world's most famous bridal-gown designer. She was born in New York City in 1949. Her parents were immigrants from China and were financially well-off. She became a fashion editor at *Vogue* magazine. When she got married in 1989, she couldn't find a bridal gown that she liked, so she decided to design her own. The next year, she opened a bridal boutique in New York City. Since then, she has gone on to design other types of women's clothes. Many movie stars wear Vera Wang dresses to movie premieres and award shows.

Sports Superstars

Baseball is not a big sport in mainland China, but it is extremely popular in Taiwan. The most successful Taiwanese player in Major League Baseball has been Chien-Ming Wang. In 2006 and 2007 he was the best pitcher on the New York Yankees, winning nineteen games in each season. After missing much of the 2008 season with an injury, he signed a new contract with the Yankees for 2009.

Another Chinese athlete who has gotten a lot of attention is basketball player Yao Ming. It's hard not to pay attention to him because he is 7 feet, 6 inches (2.3 meters) tall. He was born in Shanghai, China, in 1980. His size and skills made him an outstanding basketball player in China. In 2002, Yao became the first foreign player to be the

One Person's Story: Mina Hsing

Mina Hsing is a Chinese-American artist who lives in Evanston, Illinois. She was born in Shanghai and, as a child in China, she studied classical Chinese brush painting. When she was nineteen, her parents relocated to Brazil, and she went with them. A year after that she struck out on her own and went to New York City. She later studied art at the University of California and then got her master's degree from Mundelein College in Chicago. It was in Chicago that she met and married her husband, Peter.

She wasn't always an artist. She explains, "I worked for three years as a computer programmer, and then my children were born, so I didn't work."

She describes how she began her art career: "In the United States I was keeping up my artwork all the time. I didn't have to work. My husband worked for IBM, so there was the opportunity for me to do my artwork. So my children grew up, and I opened three galleries. Then, fifteen years later, my husband passed away. Then I started seriously to pursue my own art career." That was in 2003. "I started to see other people's work and learning what works in the market," she says. "Sometimes you paint for yourself, sometimes you paint for the market. So I do very diverse work. I do contemporary art and traditional Chinese painting. I've been living in the West for a long time," she says, "but my native voice is Chinese. I can't separate both. That's in my personality."

In 2008, Mina Hsing was teaching in a Chinese school once a week, giving students a brief introduction to brush painting. "I also go to different areas and give one-day workshops. Briefly, it's how to hold a brush, how to use a brush, what can you do with a brush. It's the magic of the brush."

Mina Hsing at a gallery with some of her paintings.

number-one pick in the draft of the National Basketball Association, and he was signed by the Houston Rockets. Yao became a huge celebrity both in the United States and in China.

Yao Ming of the Houston Rockets in action in an early 2009 game.

Michelle Kwan is one of the world's most famous ice skaters. She was born in California in 1980. Her parents were immigrants from Hong Kong. She started skating at age five and won her first figure skating competition when she was seven. When she skates, Kwan always wears a necklace that her grandmother gave her. It has a Chinese dragon and a good luck symbol on it. In 1994, when she was only thirteen years old, Kwan finished eighth in the World Championships. She won the World Championships five times between 1996 and 2003. She won a silver medal at the Olympic Winter Games in 1998 and a bronze at the 2002 Olympics. An injury kept her from competing in the 2006 Winter Olympics.

New York's Chinatown is home to many
less affluent Chinese immigrants.

CHAPTER SIX

LOOKING TO THE FUTURE

What lies ahead for the Chinese Americans? That depends on which Chinese Americans you're talking about. People who study Chinese immigration often speak of two main categories of Chinese Americans today (although, of course, in a group as large and as diverse as Chinese Americans, not all people will fit neatly into one category or the other). These two groups are often referred to as the Uptown Chinese and the Downtown Chinese.

The Uptown Chinese

The Uptown Chinese tend to be well-educated professionals who are well-off economically. A number of Uptown Chinese immigrated from or are the descendants of people who immigrated from Hong Kong or Taiwan. Those who

A Chinese-American scientist works with DNA samples in a research lab.

immigrated tended to earn high incomes before coming to the United States, and in the United States, they want to keep their high living standards. The Uptown Chinese often don't want to live in crowded center-city China-towns. They tend to look for homes in the suburbs or in suburban-like residential neighborhoods of cities. Many pick communities known to have good schools.

The Uptown Chinese often don't want to have to travel all the way to Chinatown to buy Chinese foods and other familiar products. So Chinese-American **entrepreneurs** often build and operate local supermarkets and shopping malls that cater to Chinese-American customers. In some places, whole streets become filled with businesses owned by Chinese Americans. Some suburbs with many Chinese-

American residents have Chinese newspapers and social clubs. They have Chinese-language schools, so that the children of immigrants can practice speaking their parents' native language.

In communities with growing Chinese-American populations, the new residents sometimes meet with hostility. Some people who have lived in the community for a long time don't like the changes and start to feel that they're being pushed out. Sometimes they take actions to try to block the increasing Chinese-American influence on community life. In Cupertino, California, many white residents strongly opposed a request by Chinese-American parents that the public schools start teaching Chinese. The plan to offer Chinese was ultimately approved by the local school district. But in Palo Alto, California, in 2007, the school district turned down a request to teach Chinese in the schools.

Anti-Chinese feelings aren't found only in California. A poll taken in 2001 found that, nationwide, a significant number of Americans had negative feelings about Chinese Americans. One out of four people polled said they would not want a family member to marry a Chinese American. One out of three said they felt Chinese Americans were more loyal to China than to the United States.

Perhaps at least in part to protect their rights, more Chinese Americans are going into politics and gaining political offices at all levels of government. For example, from 2002 to 2004, Chinese American Wilma Chan was the majority leader of the California state assembly. David Wu, who was born in Taiwan and came to the

Gary Locke

For Chinese Americans, November 5, 1996, was an exciting day. That was the day on which voters in the state of Washington elected Gary Locke to be their governor. Locke, a U.S.-born Chinese American, became the first Chinese-American governor in U.S. history.

Gary Locke was born in 1950. He grew up in a public housing project. His family spoke Chinese at home, and Gary didn't start speaking English until he was five. After law school, Locke worked as King County (Washington) deputy prosecutor. He then decided to go into politics. He was elected to the Washington state legislature and served for ten years. After that, he became the executive of King County, where Seattle is located.

When Locke decided to run for governor, Chinese Americans in Washington were excited and proud. But many wondered whether enough voters would support a Chinese-American politician. They didn't need to worry. Locke won easily, and he was re-elected to a second term in 2000. As governor, he helped many companies in Washington sell their products in China. Locke left office in 2005 at the end of his second term and returned to practicing law. Four years later, he became U.S. secretary of commerce in the administration of President Barack Obama.

Flanked by President Obama and Vice President Joe Biden, Gary Locke speaks at the news conference where his appointment as commerce secretary was announced.

United States with his parents as a young child, was elected to the U.S. House of Representatives from a district in Oregon in 1998; he was re-elected to a sixth term in November 2008. In 2009, Steven Chu, the American-born son of Chinese immigrants and a Nobel Prize–winning physicist, became the U.S. secretary of energy in the administration of President Barack Obama. Chinese-

American Gary Locke was governor of Washington for eight years and became U.S. secretary of commerce in 2009.

The Downtown Chinese

In contrast to the Uptown Chinese, the Downtown Chinese tend to be less well-off economically and to have less formal education. This group includes many of the undocumented immigrants who have entered the United States from China. They tend to work in lower-paying

A government official (*left*) investigates a New York Chinatown factory for using child workers.

jobs and are more likely to live in center-city Chinatowns. There are many clothing factories in Chinatowns in New York, San Francisco, Philadelphia, and other cities. Nearly all the workers are women. They operate sewing machines and other equipment. Among those who are married, the husbands often work in restaurants. These people are working long hours for low pay, and exploitation of workers in sweatshops remains a serious problem in some Chinese-American communities. For example, in 2008 the New York State Department of Labor investigated a clothing factory in New York City and found that workers were making $3.79 an hour—although state law said that the minimum wage an employer could pay workers was $7.15 an hour.

As Chinatowns have grown in population in recent decades, some Chinese Americans have been able to open small businesses that serve the Chinese-speaking population—businesses like grocery stores, real estate offices, travel agencies, and beauty salons. For the business owners, if such businesses prosper, they can be a pathway for **social mobility**: families become economically better off, can better afford to send their children to college, and have a wider range of choices as to where they can afford to live. Small businesses have often been a pathway to middle-class life for members of new immigrant groups.

But many residents of Chinatowns can afford only low-cost housing. One of the problems that Chinatowns face today is rising housing costs. A Chinatown is almost always located near the center of a city. This convenience can make such areas appealing to many people.

One Person's Story: Chao Qi

Chao Qi is an assistant professor at the Feinberg School of Medicine at Northwestern University in Chicago. She was born in what she calls the "Middle West" of mainland China. She graduated from college and got a master's degree in China, and she first came to the United States to get a doctorate. She says that she didn't really speak English until coming to the United States. "We learned English in school, but we were only able to read and write because our teachers were Chinese and were never really exposed to spoken English. I was looking for a job when I came here, and the person who interviewed me said, 'You can't speak English.'"

Her husband was born in China and finished medical school there. They met and got married in China, and they immigrated together to the United States. They have two sons, both born in the United States, whose ages were eight and two in 2008.

"Our older boy can speak Chinese," she says, "but he's not really comfortable. We speak Chinese to him at home, but he answers in English. . . . It's important for him to learn Chinese, but it's hard to force him to do that. He's in third grade in public school. It's not in a Chinese neighborhood. The third grade has only three Chinese students."

Chao Qi says that there are "a lot of differences between Chinese and American families. For example, in Chinese families at whatever level, education is considered the most important thing. . . . Chinese families . . . are famous for pushing their children too hard. Education is one thing; another thing is the traditional regard for being hard working. If you want to do well, you have to work hard. No matter how hard your job is, you have to do your best. I tell people in American families, 'you allow your children to do whatever they like to do.' We don't accept that."

Because of the cultural differences, she says, "there is like an invisible barrier between Chinese families and families of other cultures. The rules and the values are different."

Chao Qi grew up in a very controlled environment. When she was young, she spent at least ten hours a day studying. She wasn't allowed to watch TV, see movies, or play with other kids.

When she came to the United States, she says, "I had to put in extra work to catch up. When I started graduate school, I couldn't even understand what the teacher was talking about in the lecture. I had to record it and then go over it, over and over," she explains, until she could grasp the meaning. "So most of the time I had to study."

She says about her own sons: "I want [them] to receive the best education that can be offered. . . . I think that is the most important thing a parent can do for the children."

Expensive new buildings have been built, for example, in New York City's Chinatown. Some of them have apartments that cost millions of dollars to buy. Sometimes developers or individuals buy existing buildings that may not be very expensive because they are not in good condition and then fix them up; once such a building has been improved, it can be sold or rented for much more than used to be the case. This kind of change in a community's housing is part of a process called **gentrification**. Gentrification is a process in which affluent outsiders move into lower-income city neighborhoods. They improve the area, but housing prices go up. Many of the original inhabitants cannot afford to live there anymore. Besides New York, gentrification has been taking place in many other Chinatowns located in all parts of the United States, including those in San Francisco, Boston, Seattle, and Washington, D.C.

The Issues Ahead

In the coming years, Chinese Americans will likely continue to face some degree of discrimination and prejudice. Tensions within some families between the immigrant generation and their more assimilated children and grandchildren will have to be worked through. And some Chinese Americans will continue to face issues of poverty and sweatshop working conditions.

But Chinese Americans now make up a community of more than 3 million people that, overall, is well educated and reasonably well-off. The Chinese-American community in the United States has made great progress since the first immigrants landed in "Gold Mountain" more than 150 years ago. There is every reason to believe that such progress will continue and that Chinese Americans will continue to contribute in many ways to the diverse culture of the United States.

FACTS ABOUT CHINESE AMERICANS

Characteristic	Chinese Americans	Percentage for Chinese Americans	Total U.S. Population	Percentage for U.S. Population
Total population	3,090,453		299,398,485	
Male	1,483,417	48%	146,705,258	49%
Female	1,607,036	52%	152,693,227	51%
Median age (years)	37		36	
Under 5 years old	185,427	6%	20,957,894	7%
18 years and over	2,444,146	79%	224,548,864	75%
65 years and over	339,950	11%	35,927,818	12%
Average family size	3		3	
Number of households	1,029,424		111,617,402	
Owner-occupied housing units	648,537	63%	74,783,659	67%
Renter-occupied housing units	380,887	37%	36,833,743	33%
People age 25 and over with high school diploma or higher	1,766,317	82%	164,729,046	84%
People age 25 and over with bachelor's degree or higher	1,120,104	52%	52,948,622	27%
Foreign born	2,153,038	70%	37,547,789	13%
Number of people who speak a language other than English at home (population 5 years and older)	2,427,787	83%	55,807,878	20%
Median family income	$75,245		$58,526	
Per capita income	$29,189		$25,267	
Individuals living below the poverty level	370,854	12%	38,921,803	13%

Source: U.S. Bureau of the Census, 2006 American Community Survey estimates

GLOSSARY

acupuncture: An ancient Chinese healing practice; it is a way of deadening pain or of changing certain body conditions by inserting fine needles into the skin.

affluent: Economically well-off.

assimilation: The process by which people who have moved to another country adopt the customs and behaviors of the people in their new environment.

Communists: Followers of a political and economic system in which a powerful government closely controls people's activities and centrally plans a country's economy.

discrimination: Unfair treatment of a person or group based on such characteristics such as race, ethnic group, or religion.

documented immigrant: An immigrant who has official government documents, such as a visa, that give him or her permission to live, study, or work in the United States permanently or for a period of time.

entrepreneur: Someone who starts, supplies the money for, and operates a new business.

extended family: Family members besides parents and their unmarried children; extended family members may include grandparents, married children and their spouses, aunts and uncles, and others.

feng shui: An ancient Chinese art of arranging objects in a room or other space to create harmony and balance.

gentrification: A process in which economically better-off outsiders move into a lower-income city neighborhood, often displacing the previous inhabitants.

immigrant visa: A document issued by the U.S. government allowing the person receiving it to live and work permanently in the United States.

kung fu: An ancient Chinese art of self-defense.

prejudice: Negative judgments about a person or a group based on such things as race, religion, ethnic group, or economic status.

refugee: Someone who seeks or takes shelter in a foreign country, especially to avoid war, political persecution, or religious persecution in his or her native country.

sea turtles: Chinese people living in the United States who decide to return to China.

snakeheads: People who smuggle undocumented Chinese immigrants into the United States.

social mobility: The opportunity for people to improve their economic situation and way of life.

stereotype: A commonly held idea about the characteristics of an entire group of people. Stereotypes do not take into consideration the individual differences among people belonging to any group.

sweatshop: A factory in which laborers work long hours for low pay, often in a difficult or even dangerous working environment.

temporary visa: A U.S. government document that grants permission for a person to come to the United States for a fixed period of time, for example, to study at a university.

undocumented immigrant: An immigrant who enters and remains in the United States without obtaining the permission and paperwork required by U.S. law.

TO FIND OUT MORE

Further Reading

Anderson, Dale. *Chinese Americans*. Milwaukee, WI: World Almanac Library, 2007.

Lingen, Marissa K. *Chinese Immigration*. Philadelphia: Mason Crest, 2004.

Martin, Michael. *Chinese Americans*. Philadelphia: Chelsea House, 2003.

Perl, Lila. *To the Golden Mountain: The Story of Chinese Who Built the Railroad*. New York: Marshall Cavendish Benchmark, 2003.

Shane, C. J. *The Chinese*. Detroit, MI: Thomson Gale, 2005.

Websites

http://online.sfsu.edu/~ericmar/catimeline.html
From San Francisco State University, a detailed Chinese American History Timeline from 1848 to 1965.

http://www.asianamerican.net
An Internet resource with information about Asian Americans for students, teachers, and businesspeople.

http://www.ccamuseum.org
This website of the Chinese-American Museum of Chicago offers a wide-ranging series of scholarly papers dealing with Chinese-American history.

http://www.chcp.org
This website of the Chinese Historical and Cultural Project (CHCP) has a Virtual Museum & Library that includes a great deal of information on Chinese culture.

http://www.ocanational.org
This website of the Organization of Chinese Americans features a comprehensive report entitled "A Portrait of Chinese Americans."

http://www.pbs.org/becomingamerican
This Public Broadcasting Service website to accompany a TV special includes eyewitness accounts of the Chinese-American experience, portraits of Chinese Americans, and an interview with Maya Lin.

BIBLIOGRAPHY

The author found these sources especially helpful when researching this volume:

"A Land Squeeze in America's Chinatowns." *The Christian Science Monitor*, July 10, 2007.

"Chinese Cuisine in the United States." http://www.lifeintheusa.com/food/chinese.htm.

Jung, John. *Chinese Laundries: Tickets to Survival on Gold Mountain*. Lulu.com, 2007.

Kwong, Peter, and Dusanka Miscevic. *Chinese America: The Untold Story of America's Oldest New Community*. New York: The New Press, 2005.

Lai, David Chuenyan. "The Visual Character of Chinatowns." *Places: Forum of Design for the Public Realm*, Vol. 7, Issue 1, October 1990. http://repositories.cdlib.org/ced/places/vol7/iss1/DavidChuenyanLai.

Limerick, Patricia Nelson. "Witnesses to Persecution." *New York Times*, July 29, 2007.

Liu, Melinda, and Duncan Hewitt. "Rise of the Sea Turtles: China's Most Modern Citizens Aren't Drawing It Any Closer to the West." *Newsweek*, August 9, 2008. http://www.newsweek.com/id/151730.

"A Portrait of Chinese Americans." The Organization of Chinese Americans (OCA). http://www.ocanational.org.

Tung, May Paomay. *Chinese Americans and Their Immigrant Parents*. New York: The Haworth Clinical Practice Press, 2000.

Tung, William L. *The Chinese in America, 1820–1973: A Chronology & Fact Book*. Dobbs Ferry, NY: Oceana Publications, 1974.

Wong, Christy. "Being Chinese American and Embracing the 'Twinkie.'" ChicagoTribune.com, June 25, 2008. http://newsblogs.chicagotribune.com/race/2008/06/being-chinese-a.html.

The author conducted personal interviews with the following people quoted in this book, and the author and the publisher wish to thank them for their cooperation:

Zhen (Tony) Wu
Mina Hsing
Chao Qi

All websites were accessible as of March 25, 2009.

INDEX

Page numbers in **boldface** are illustrations, tables, and charts.

About the Series Consultant

Judith Ann Warner is a Professor of Sociology and Criminal Justice at Texas A&M International University (TAMIU), located in Laredo, Texas, near the U.S.-Mexico border. She has specialized in the study of race and ethnic relations, focusing on new immigrants to the United States and their social incorporation into American society. Professor Warner is the editor of and contributed a number of essays to *Battleground Immigration* (2009), a collection of essays on immigration and related national security issues. Recognition of her work includes the 2007 Distance Educator of the Year Award and the 1991 Scholar of the Year Award at TAMIU.

About the Author

Joseph Gustaitis is a freelance writer and editor living in Chicago. He has a doctorate in history from Columbia University in New York City and has been the author of many articles in the popular history field. After working as an editor at *Collier's Year Book*, he became the humanities editor for *Collier's Encyclopedia*. He has also worked in television and won an Emmy Award for writing for ABC-TV's *FYI* program. This is his first book for Marshall Cavendish Benchmark.